DUTCH COOKING
THE NEW KITCHEN

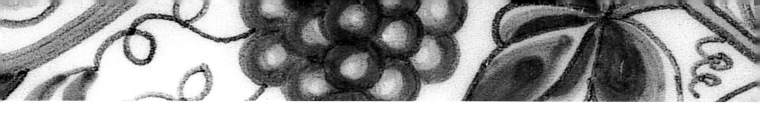

Becht · Haarlem

DUTCH COOKING
THE NEW KITCHEN

Manon Sikkel
Michiel Klønhammer

Second Edition, 2004

Translated into English by: World Wide Translations (Steve Cranko)
© 2003 Manon Sikkel and Michiel Klønhammer
For this publication:
© 2003 Uitgeverij J.H. Gottmer / H.J.W. Becht BV, Postbus 317, 2000 AH Haarlem (e-mail: post@gottmer.nl)
Publisher: Uitgeverij J.H. Gottmer / H.J.W. Becht BV is part of the Gottmer Uitgevers Groep BV
Photography: Gerhard Witteveen, Apeldoorn
Cover design and interior: Jan Brands, Bureau voor Grafische Vormgeving, 's-Hertogenbosch
Printing: Drukkerij Wilco, Amersfoort

ISBN 90 230 1127 9 / NUR 442

*We have fond memories of our grandmothers, Anna Minderman and Cornelia Troost.
Two fantastic women who knew how to cook like nobody else. It was with great pleasure that we adapted their family recipes to our way of cooking.*

Contents

The Dutch kitchen

Dutch cooking does not, to say the least, have a very good international reputation. Friends from abroad who visit us in the Netherlands treasure fond memories of croquettes, chocolate sprinkles and treacle waffles. Yet they hardly ever ask for directions to a Dutch restaurant, or, when they are here they stick to a visit to an Indonesian restaurant. When writing this book we heard an influential *New York Times* restaurant critic say: '*The Dutch don't have a kitchen, they have food*'. During a recent visit the French world-class chef Paul Bocuse called the Netherlands 'a culinary desert'.

A culinary desert

Worst of all is that the Dutch themselves are not particularly proud of their own kitchen. When reading a traditional cookbook from the Netherlands, one can't help but notice that little attention is paid to detail. The main quality of many recipes is perhaps that Dutch food is generally nutritious and cheap and that the Dutch eat a relatively large amount of vegetables. But often little attention is paid to subtle tastes, vegetables are cooked too long and fresh herbs are hardly used.
Although the Dutch still cook traditionally most of the time, they consider their own kitchen especially suitable for weekday meals. During the weekends they gladly enjoy recipes from other countries.

The Dutch are often prejudiced against the taste of 'old fashioned' vegetables like beetroot, Brussels sprouts and turnips. Because of their enormous interest in other kitchens they have often forgotten what salsify, kohlrabi or purslane taste like, and, oddly enough, no one seems to experiment with typical Dutch dishes, like 'stamppot' (vegetable and potato mash), while there's still so much to be discovered.

Meat, vegetables and potatoes

Although the Dutch kitchen may originally have been a simple one, a rich choice of meat and vegetables has always been available, so there is no lack of ingredients to fulfill the traditional need for meat, vegetables and potatoes.
Many products available in the Netherlands have however — perhaps due to our frugal disposition — not been of very high quality during the last few decades. Fortunately, in recent years, better meat and vegetables have become available. The Dutch tomato, for example, was for years infamous for its lack of taste; nowadays it is easier to buy really tasty ones. Hopefully, the rumours that the tomatoes exported to Germany are packed in crates without the label 'Made in Holland' will at some stage disappear.

Not only has the quality of vegetables improved recently, the appearance of organic meat has had a positive influence on the quality of meat.

Potatoes seem to have always been known in the Netherlands. The Netherlands only became a potato country in the seventeenth century. Before then the parsnip was the main ingredient for many recipes, until the potato was introduced – never to disappear again. Vegetables used to be scarce in the winter and as a result a lot of preserving took place at the end of summer. Vegetables and fruits disappeared into preserving jars, pickled, salted, and in jams. The potato, originally from South America, was available all winter long and was excellent for masking the strong tastes of preserved meats and vegetables.

The potato is still highly appreciated, in spite of competition from pasta, rice and couscous. New potato products continue to be introduced today, including organically grown potatoes and numerous new varieties.

Spices

The colonial past brought a wealth of spices to the Netherlands, like pepper, nutmeg and cinnamon. They were all non-perishable, and were avidly traded. When the Dutch think about the Golden Age they often envisage warehouses 'bulging' with enormous amounts of spices. Pepper was more a currency than a culinary ingredient. It is striking to see that many of the herbs that originate in countries much closer like France and Italy have only become really popular during recent decades. First the dried French and Italian herbs made their entry into the Dutch kitchen and only very recently did fresh herbs become more common, something we are very pleased about.

The new Dutch kitchen

So what is the new Dutch kitchen? Many of the dishes dealt with here can be traced back to centuries-old Dutch cookbooks. Many dishes are familiar to us because our grandmothers cooked them. Although we loved our grandmothers very much and have adopted their passion for cooking, we still have memories of overcooked vegetables, obligatory sauces and plenty of greasy gravy.

The Dutch have only recently started to experiment with their own kitchen. Up to now we preferred to turn to exotic kitchens like the Indonesian, Thai or Mexican for new influences. Who would ever try something new with grandmother's food? Traditional recipes were left alone, even when there was room for improvement. Organic cooking and the increased appreciation for locally produced seasonal vegetables have contributed to a renewed interest in our own, traditional recipes.

The crux of our view on the new Dutch kitchen is that we should respect the ingredienst we cook with (demand a tomato with taste!) and use more fresh ingredients, but also be flexible with the methods of preparation. In this book we stick to certain herbs and spices that are typical to Dutch cooking, like bay leaves, nutmeg, cinnamon and freshly ground pepper, but we also add generous amounts of fresh herbs (use them by the handfuls!) and we think that garlic is a must for many recipes. We also show that Dutch dishes like pea soup, hotch potch and stew with rucola can be prepared excellently without meat, though we also know how to enjoy a meatball and hash.
We have also adjusted cooking times and herbs considerably compared to traditional recipes. Important for the new Dutch kitchen is that almost all cooking times are shorter than in the past (that's, tastier, healthier, and quicker) and that we don't always stick to often unnecessary traditions like peeling potatoes. If our grandmothers only knew...

N.B. All recipes are for four people unless otherwise stated.

Vegetable calendar

This vegetable calendar gives an overview of the harvesting times for Dutch vegetables that are grown outside or in unheated greenhouses. We didn't include some vegetables like French beans as they nearly always come from abroad and are often flown in by airplane. Greenhouse produce and vegetables that are flown in cost much more energy and are bad for the environment (which doesn't mean that they don't taste better that our out of season local produce). Actually we prefer Spanish tomatoes compared to the sad tomato plant we have in our windowsill any day, but that's beside the point.

JANUARY
kale
leek
salsify
Savoy cabbage
lamb's lettuce
winter purslane

FEBRUARY
kale
leek
salsify
Savoy cabbage
lamb's lettuce
winter purslane

MARCH
broccoli
kale
lamb's lettuce
leek
salsify
spinach
Swiss chard
winter purslane

APRIL
asparagus
broccoli
cabbage lettuce
cauliflower
endive
kohlrabi
leek
rhubarb
spinach
Swiss chard
turnip tops
watercress

MAY
asparagus
broccoli
cabbage lettuce
cauliflower
conical cabbage
endive
kohlrabi
leek
legumes
rhubarb
spinach

spring onion
Swiss chard
turnip tops
watercress

JUNE
asparagus
broad beans
broccoli
cabbage lettuce
cauliflower
Chinese cabbage
conical cabbage
endive
garden peas
kohlrabi
leek
legumes
rhubarb
Savoy cabbage
spinach
spring onion
Swiss chard
turnip tops
watercress

JULY

eet root
blanched celery
broad beans
broccoli
cabbage lettuce
cauliflower
Chinese cabbage
conical cabbage
courgette
endive
fennel
garden peas
haricot beans
iceberg lettuce
kohlrabi
leek
legumes
red cabbage
Savoy cabbage
spinach
spring onion
Swiss chard
watercress
white cabbage

AUGUST

beet root
blanched celery
broad beans
broccoli
cabbage lettuce
cauliflower
celeriac
Chinese cabbage

conical cabbage
courgette
endive
fennel
haricot beans
iceberg lettuce
kohlrabi
leek
legumes
pumpkin
red cabbage
Savoy cabbage
spinach
spring onion
Swiss chard
watercress
white cabbage

SEPTEMBER

beet root
blanched celery
broad beans
broccoli
cabbage lettuce
cauliflower
celeriac
Chinese cabbage
conical cabbage
courgette
endive
fennel
haricot beans
iceberg lettuce
kohlrabi
leek

pumpkin
red cabbage
Savoy cabbage
spinach
Swiss chard
watercress
white cabbage
winter carrot
winter radish

OCTOBER

beet root
blanched celery
broccoli
cabbage lettuce
cauliflower
celeriac
Chinese cabbage
conical cabbage
courgette
endive
fennel
haricot beans
iceberg lettuce
kale
kohlrabi
lamb's lettuce
leek
pumpkin
red cabbage
salsify
Savoy cabbage
spinach
Swiss chard
swee

white cabbage
winter carrot
winter radish

NOVEMBER

broccoli
cabbage lettuce
cauliflower
celeriac
Chinese cabbage
endive
kale
lamb's lettuce
leek
salsify
Savoy cabbage
swede
white cabbage
winter radish

DECEMBER

kale
lamb's lettuce
leek
salsify
Savoy cabbage
winter purslane

Note: celeriac, swedes, pumpkin, winter radish, beetroot, red cabbage, winter carrot, and onions are also available in the months afterwards as they can be kept for a long time
Source: Milieu Centraal and Productschap Tuinbouw

Soups

From way back, the Dutch kitchen has been known for its rather substantial and nutritious soups. Pea soup – 'Dutch pea soup' as the Dutch call it – is the most famous of all. We of course prefer to eat it after the iceskating, in the afterglow of the fun, at the stands serving food and drink on the edge of a frozen lake or canal. Understandable, but the soup served is not usually fresh. A pity because making your own soup is one of the funnest things there is.

Cheese soup
Kaassoep

We are privileged to have a choice of fantastic cheeses in the Netherlands, most of which are suitable for soup. Although a cheese soup recipe appears every now and then in some older Dutch cookbooks, it usually doesn't consist of much more than an unseasoned mixture of flour and cheese. It's a piece of cake to turn this basic recipe into an easily prepared delicacy. For cheese soup, several types of Dutch cheese are suitable. Ordinary old cheese (not the extremely old kind as that's to dry) is our favourite.

Ingredients

1 onion
2 cloves of garlic
2 tablespoons olive oil
25 grams butter
25 grams flour
1 litre vegetable stock
250 grams grated 'old' cheese ('oude kaas')
a handful of flat-leaf parsley
100 ml dry white wine
1 dl sour cream
a handful of chives
salt and freshly grounded black pepper

Chop the onion and garlic into small pieces. Lightly brown the onion and the garlic in the olive oil in a soup pot. Add the butter and let it melt. Add the flour and pour in the stock, stirring to a thin smooth sauce.

Add the cheese, with the finely chopped flat-leaf parsley and the wine. Let it heat through for a few minutes and then stir in the sour cream. Make sure that the cheese melts properly and that it doesn't sink to the bottom. Taste to see if it needs salt.
Serve the cheese soup with plenty of chopped chives and freshly ground black pepper.

Pea soup
Erwtensoep

Ingredients

TRADITIONAL PEA SOUP

400 grams shoulder chops
500 grams green split peas
2 ½ litres water
2 bay leaves
1 leek
1 winter carrot
150 grams smoked bacon
1 smoked sausage (250 gr)
    (rookworst)
250 grams
salt
freshly ground black pepper

Ingredients

VEGETARIAN PEA SOUP

500 grams green split peas
2 ½ litres water
2 bay leaves
500 grams celeriac
2 onions
1 leek
50 grams butter
1 courgette
1 fennel
1 winter carrot
1 stalk flat-leaf parsley
chives
salt
freshly ground pepper

According to traditional recipes, pea soup consists of almost more meat than peas. This recipe was originally prepared with pig's trotters, bacon and smoked sausage. Nothing wrong with that, but we prefer shoulder chops. A vegetarian pea soup can also be delicious. That's why we've given a recipe for both a substantial meaty variety as well as one of our favourite vegetarian soups. Pea soup is usually rather thick. Dutch people say that if the spoon remains standing upright then the soup is good, however we also enjoy a more liquid pea soup.

Cut the shoulder chops in pieces, add water and bring to the boil. Turn down the heat to a simmer. Add bay leaves and salt. Scoop off the froth that forms while cooking a number of times.
Cut the leek into pieces and wash it. Cut the carrot into large slices and after half an hour add it and the leek to the soup.
Dice the bacon and add this to the soup as well. Allow it to boil for one and a half hours. Add water if necessary and add salt and pepper to taste.
Just before serving, add the entire sausage to warm it up. Remove the sausage, cut it into slices and divide these among the plates of soup. You really do justice to the soup by letting it cool down completely and then heating it up again just before serving.

Vegetarian

Rinse the split peas, add water and bring to the boil. Add two tablespoons of salt and the bay leaves. Cut the celeriac into pieces and add it to the soup. When boiling scoop off the froth a few times.

Cut the onion and leek into pieces and sauté them in a frying pan with the butter. Add some more salt while frying. Add the pieces of onion and leek to the boiling soup after half an hour. Cut the courgette and the fennel into small pieces and the carrot into thick slices and add all of this to the soup as well.

Let the soup boil for about an hour and a half. Add some water if necessary. Add the finely chopped parsley towards the end and season the soup with pepper and salt. Garnish with chives.

Leek and potato soup
Aardappel-preisoep

The Dutch are potato eaters, and as potato eaters they naturally also eat potato soup, often filled with leek, bacon or celeriac. Entire families had to feed themselves with this soup for days; and as soup is only really tasty if you make plenty – It's always nicer the next day – we provide a recipe for six servings. Or for four hard-working farmers who have been in the fields all day.

Ingredients
(6 servings)
1 kilo floury potatoes
1 winter carrot
2 leeks
5 dl of milk
25 grams butter
1 bundle flat-leaf parsley (50 grams)
$1/2$ a nutmeg
a knob of butter
white wine vinegar
1 spring onion
pepper
salt

Peel the potatoes, wash them and cut them into eighths.
Scrape the carrot and cut it into slices.

Cut the leeks into rings and wash them.

Heat a knob of butter in the pot and gently simmer the leeks for a few minutes.

Bring a litre and a half of water to the boil. Add the potatoes, leeks, carrots and quite a bit of salt. Bring to the boil again and allow to simmer for another 25 minutes.

Heat the milk and the butter in a pan. Chop the flat-leaf parsley and add it to the milk with the ground nutmeg, some freshly ground black pepper and salt. Add one or two tablespoons of white wine vinegar. Pour the mixture into the soup and let it simmer for another 15 minutes.

Garnish with rings of spring onion.

Eel and asparagus soup
Soep van paling en asperges

Asparagus and eels are important elements of the Dutch culinary tradition. But they are rarely eaten together. This soup shows that the combination actually works very well. Nowadays you can buy asparagus all year round in the Netherlands; they are however tastiest in asparagus season (mid April to June). Connoisseurs know that eel should be eaten between May and December. For both eels and asparagus, our advice is: buy thin ones. Thick asparagus are rather rough and thick eels are very fatty.

White asparagus have to be peeled first. Cut a piece off the bottom of either white or green asparagus. Cut them into pieces about 5 cm long.
Boil the asparagus with a little salt in half a litre of water for 15-20 minutes. Green asparagus will be cooked in 5 to 10 minutes.

Meanwhile, bring the white wine to the boil in a separate pot and add the eel, the chopped garlic, the bay leaves and the large chunks of carrot and onion.
Strain the wine after 10 minutes. Save the eel and discard the onion and carrot.

Cut the eel into 5 cm pieces and add these and the wine to the asparagus. Add the cream and taste the soup. Add salt and lavish with freshly ground pepper.

Ingredients

300 grams asparagus (preferably
   green ones)
250 ml white wine
300 grams eel fillets
1 clove of garlic
2 bay leaves
1 large carrot
1 onion
100 ml cream
freshly ground black pepper
salt

Potato

Potatoes are still incredibly popular in the Netherlands although we don't eat as much of them as we used to. The Dutch still eat about 81 kilos each a year. Almost half of this is bought unpeeled. The remainder is consumed in the form of chips and other potato products. The 'bintje' used to be the most famous Dutch potato, but it has lost much of its popularity. Relatively large amounts of pesticides are necessary to grow 'bintjes' as they're quite susceptible to potato diseases. Environmental organisations have even managed to ban the 'bintje' from some shops to the great dissatisfaction of the potato industry. Luckily there's still plenty of choice from stronger varieties.

Houses of Amsterdam
Amsterdamse huisjes

If you've ever been to Amsterdam you'll know that may houses look like they're about to fall over (sometimes they do!). So you shouldn't be embarrassed if this delicious potato dish doesn't stay upright on your plate, though you should try. This dish – in all its simplicity – demands really good cheese, preferably matured farm cheese, and tasty firm onions or shallots.

Ingredients
8 large potatoes (firm cookers)
5 shallots or 2 firm onions
150 grams mature farm cheese ('belegen boerenkaas')
pepper
salt

Peel the potatoes and cut them into rectangular blocks by cutting off the sides and ends (these you should of course keep for tomorrow's hotchpotch!).
Boil these rectangular potatoes for about 10 minutes. Then drain them and cut them into thin slices.

Preheat the oven to 250 °C.

Grease a baking dish. Build the houses by putting a slice of potato in the greased baking dish with an onion ring and a slice of cheese on top of it. Put a new slice of potato on top of that and keep building in the same order until you have used up the potato. If it really doesn't keep standing, then insert a small skewer into the potato stack from the top.

Put the baking dish in the oven for about 10 minutes until the cheese has melted. Remove the houses from the baking dish or put very carefully the entire dish on the table and leave this difficult task to your guests.

Celeriac and potato mash
Knolselderijstamppot

Celeriac isn't only cheap and healthy, it's also great for soups, salads and potato mashes. You should always make Dutch potato mash in large quantities as it will taste even better a day or two later.

Bring a pot with ample water to the boil.

Peel the potatoes and cut them into large chunks.

Peel the celeriac and cut into large blocks.

Add the potatoes and the celeriac to the boiling water with a pinch of salt and cook for 20 minutes.

Slice the onions and put them in a pan with the knob of butter and the sugar. Braise for ten minutes on a low heat.

Heat the cream with the nutmeg, the mustard, and some salt and pepper in a saucepan.

Drain the potatoes and the celeriac and mix in the warm cream and onions. Mash everything with a masher and season with pepper and salt. Use a wooden spoon if you don't own a Dutch potato masher.

Serve with smoked sausage or some slices of cheese.

Tip You can use milk instead of cream.

Ingredients

(6 servings)
2 kilos floury potatoes
2 celeriac (about ½ kilo)
5 onions
a knob of butter
1 teaspoon sugar
2 dl cream
1 teaspoon ground nutmeg
2 tablespoons mustard
pepper
salt

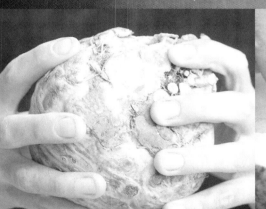

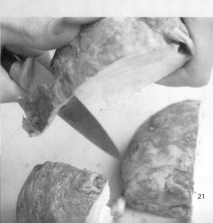

Rucola and cashew potato mash
Stamppot van rucola en cashewnoten

In recent years you can hardly enter a Dutch restaurant without being
served a plate of rucola. All our friends turned out to be rucola-fans.
So why not try a rucola hotchpotch? Other names for rucola are
rocket, roquette salad or arugula.

Ingredients
1 ½ kilos floury potatoes
200 grams rucola
200 grams cashews
butter
2 onions
2 cloves of garlic
0.5 dl milk
2 tablespoons mustard
chives
pepper
salt

Peel the potatoes, quarter them and boil them for 20 minutes in a pot with ample water and a pinch of salt.

Wash the rucola and slice it thinly.

Heat up a frying pan and roast the cashews. Keep moving them with a wooden spoon to avoid burning. Put them on a plate after a few minutes.

Cut the onion and garlic into small pieces.

Melt a knob of butter in the pan and brown the onions and garlic.

Drain the potatoes and add the cashews, onions, garlic, milk, mustard and a knob of butter. Add the sliced rucola and mash it all together. Season with pepper and salt and garnish with some fresh chives.

Serve immediately.

Hotchpotch
Hutspot

The name hotchpotch in Dutch is 'hutspot' which originates form the word hustle pot, a centuries-old dish that the Dutch learned from the Spanish occupying force during the relief of Leyden in 1574. More than four centuries later we're still eating this meatless hotchpotch – and enjoying it very much.

Wash the potatoes and peel the carrots. Peel the onions. Quarter the potatoes (they don't need to be peeled) and cut the carrots and onions into large chunks. Bring a pot with 1 litre of water to the boil. Add the potatoes in the pot, next the carrots and then the onion. Cover and boil for about 25 minutes with a teaspoon of salt, 1 teaspoon of freshly ground pepper and the bay leaves.

Pour off the water, remove the bay leaves and mash the hotchpotch with a masher. Leave some coarse chunks – it should definitely not become a soft mush. Mix in the butter and the milk and season with pepper and salt.

Chop the parsley and dice the cheese; add this just before serving.

Ingredients

1 ¹/₂ kilos potatoes
1 ¹/₂ kilos winter carrots
750 grams onions
3 bay leaves
50 grams butter
1 dl milk
a bunch of flat-leaf parsley
400 grams mature cheese
salt
black pepper

'Hete bliksem' (Hot lightning)

'Hete bliksem' or hot lightning is a term used in the northern province of Groningen to indicate both beautiful women and a hotchpotch made with apple, smoked bacon and plenty of pepper (hence the name). We like to use a combination of sweet and sour apples, but if you have to choose, use sour ones like Golden Reinettes. These will remain firmer and add more texture. The potatoes can be either floury or firm cookers.

Peel the potatoes and cut them into thick slices. Quarter every slice.

Peel the apples. Remove the cores and cut them into eighths.

Put the stock in a large pot, add the potatoes and place the apples on top.
The potatoes should be completely covered by the stock but the apples should be free. Boil the potatoes for about 25 minutes with the lid on. Remove from the stove, add pepper and salt and mix everything thoroughly. Do not mash; the dish tastes best when the apples have not completely fallen apart. Season with the butter and some salt and pepper.
Cut the bacon strips and fry them on a high flame. Serve the 'hete bliksem' with strips of bacon on top.

Ingredients

1 ^{1}/2 kilo potatoes
1 kilo sour apples (Golden
    Reinettes)
500 grams sweet apples (Golden
    Delicious)
4 dl beef stock
40 grams butter
300 grams smoked bacon (one
    piece or slices)
salt
black pepper

Main Courses

In the past foreigners were surprised by the Dutch custom of sitting down for dinner at the stroke of six. Stranger still were the measured-out amounts of potatoes, meat and vegetables so that an unexpected guest could never pull up a chair and join in. Although the Dutch still do not pay surprise visits around dinnertime, our evening meals have luckily begun to show a little more variety – partly the result of influences from abroad.

Croquettes with fresh herbs
Kroketten met verse kruiden

Ingredients

(for 8 large croquettes)

1 carrot

1 onion

2 cloves of garlic

4 bay leaves

celery leaf, a handful

400 grams stewing steak

50 grams butter

75 grams flour

fresh basil, a handful

chives, a handful

100 grams bread crumbs

1 egg

at least 750 ml (sunflower) oil for
   frying

half a head of iceberg lettuce

bread

mustard

fresh peppercorns

salt

It is not very common these days to find croquettes in an upmarket restaurant or to eat them at someone's home for dinner. One of our grandmothers used to make them herself and they were considered a real delicacy. The fun thing about a croquette is that it's so easy to create your own variations.

Fill a pot with 500 ml of water, 2 teaspoons of salt, a couple of peppercorns, the carrot, the peeled onion, cut in half, a clove of garlic, the bay leaves and the celery leaf. Add the meat (don't cut it up yet) and let it boil on a high flame. We like croquettes with the meat still firm, so we only let it cook for about half an hour, though the meat shouldn't be too tough. You can safely let it cook a little longer if it is still too tough.

Take the meat out of the broth, separate it from the vegetables and cut it into small pieces. The vegetables can be discarded. Reserve 400 ml of stock (add water if necessary).

Chop a clove of garlic and fry it a little in butter using a small sauce pan. Add the flower and pour in the stock while stirring so that you get a smooth ragout. Now add the meat and bring to a quick boil.

Remove the ragout from the stove and add the chopped basil and chives.

Pour the mixture into a flat dish and place in the fridge until it has cooled completely. Divide the stew into eight equal portions and take out four plates. Sprinkle the bread crumbs onto one plate. Beat the egg in the second plate. Use the third plate to put the croquettes on and put some paper towels on the fourth plate for when they have been fried.

Scoop a serving of stew from the dish with a large spoon, use a second spoon to roughly shape a croquette and roll it through the bread crumbs. Roll the croquette on a flat surface and flatten the ends. Roll the croquette through the egg and then again through the bread crumbs. Then carefully put it on the third plate.

Heat the oil on a medium flame (150 °C) and fry the croquettes until they are golden brown.
Serve with bread, iceberg lettuce and mustard.

Meatball roll
Broodje bal

A meatball roll is obligatory for most butchers in the Netherlands. A butcher who takes pride in his profession manages to create a tasty meatball, but more often than not one is confronted with an insipid meatball that is best drenched in as much sauce as possible. Always the answer to real hunger, but not very refined. There are a number of rules for a good Dutch meatball: it should be covered in breadcrumbs, bread should be added to the meat and it must contain nutmeg. But what stops us from adding onion, garlic, fresh rosemary and parsley? Traditional recipes required large quantities of butter and often a spoonful of tomato paste. But with a little less butter and fresh tomatoes this meatball surpasses all expectations.

Chop the onion and cut the garlic in small pieces. Put half of this aside with half of the rosemary.

Mix the minced meat with the other half of the rosemary, the onion and the garlic. Soak the bread in the milk, squeeze it out and knead it through the minced meat with the eggs, nutmeg and some pepper and salt.

Make four nice round balls with this mixture and roll them through some breadcrumbs.

Put a casserole on the fire and lightly brown the remainder of the onion, garlic and rosemary in butter. Roll the balls though the butter and fry them lightly all around, over a medium-high heat. Now turn down the stove a little, add the chopped tomatoes and let the meatballs simmer for about 20 minutes more.

Serve the meatballs on a fresh roll with a spoonful of the tomato sauce. Delicious!

Ingredients

2 cloves of garlic

1 onion

2 tablespoons fresh rosemary

500 grams minced meat

2 slices stale white bread

1 cup of milk

2 eggs

1 teaspoon nutmeg

breadcrumbs

butter

400 grams canned peeled
   tomatoes or good quality fresh
   tomatoes

pepper

salt

Bacon pancakes with avocado mousse
Spekpannenkoeken met avocadomousse

Pancakes used to be everyday food in the Netherlands. Farmers used to eat them in the morning after milking the cows. Because farming the land was hard work, the farmer's wife would add some bacon to the batter as well. A real Dutch bacon pancake should be eaten with syrup, but rolled up with steamed vegetables and avocado is of course also a possibility.

Mix the yeast in a bowl with some lukewarm milk. Put the flour in a bowl and stir in the yeast, the beaten eggs, the salt and half the milk. Stir as long as it takes to make a smooth batter, while still stirring pour in the remainder of the milk. Cover the batter with a damp cloth and leave it to rise for half an hour.

Peel the avocados and mash them with a fork. Pour the lemon juice over it and stir in the mayonnaise. Press out the garlic and mix it into the mousse. Season with salt and freshly ground pepper.

Bring a pot with 1 litre of water to the boil.

Ingredients

10 grams dry yeast
500 grams wheat flour
2 eggs
1 teaspoon salt
9 dl lukewarm milk
2 ripe avocados
juice of $\frac{1}{2}$ lemon
1 tablespoon mayonnaise
1 clove of garlic
300 grams broccoli
1 small fennel
150 grams bacon (or more)
butter
salt
pepper

Cut the broccoli florets loose. Cut the green off the fennel and then cut the fennel into small pieces. Put the broccoli and the fennel in a steamer or sieve above the pot with boiling water. Put the lid on and let the vegetables steam for 15-20 minutes.

Cut the bacon into thin strips. Heat a frying pan on high and melt a knob of butter. Fry the bacon for about 1 minute and put it aside on a plate.

Melt a knob of butter in the frying pan and pour some batter into the pan. Add some fried bacon. As soon as the bottom is done, turn the pancake and fry the other side. Keep the pancake warm and fry the rest of the pancakes.

Spread avocado mousse on the pancakes and add some broccoli and fennel on top. Roll up the pancake and serve immediately.

Cheese-garlic croquettes
Kaas-knoflookkroketten

A vegetarian croquette is very rare in the Netherlands. It doesn't make sense to leave out the meat from a meat croquette because then you take away all the flavour. Cheese works much better, especially with garlic and herbs. A cheese croquette is a little bit more difficult to prepare than a meat croquette because the cheese goes soft when deep-frying. Make sure you cover the croquettes properly with breadcrumbs and only deep-fry them for a very short time.

Ingredients

(for 8 small croquettes)

2 cloves of garlic

olive oil

25 grams butter

30 grams flour

200 ml milk

200 grams grated mature cheese

a handful of finely chopped flat-leaf parsley (or other fresh herbs)

100 grams bread crumbs

1 egg

750 ml (sunflower) oil for frying

Finely chop a clove of garlic and fry it in a little olive oil in a small sauce pan. Add the butter and the flour and mix. Add the milk slowly, stirring, so that you get a thin smooth sauce. Add the grated cheese and the parsley and let the mixture bubble for a bit until the cheese has melted completely.

Pour the mixture onto a soup plate and refrigerate. Keep refrigerated until the cheese mixture has turned into a firm, somewhat rubber-like mush. This will take at least half an hour, but the mixture may be left for longer.

Meanwhile, put out four plates. Sprinkle the breadcrumbs onto a plate. Beat the egg in the second plate. Use the third plate to put the croquettes on and put some paper towels on the fourth plate for when they have been fried.

Cut the cheese mixture into eight equal wedges. Lift a wedge from the plate with a wet spoon and use the other spoon to mould it as much as possible into the shape of a croquette. Next, roll it carefully on a flat surface for a moment and push the ends a little. Roll the croquette through the bread crumbs, then through the egg and then once more through the bread crumbs. Carefully place the croquette onto the plate.

Heat the oil on a medium flame (150 °C). Don't make it too hot, because then the croquettes will burst. Fry four at a time until golden brown and let them drip out on a paper towel.

Serve as a side dish or with bread and mustard.

Hash
Hachee

Hash is stewed meat that owes its characteristic taste to typically Dutch spices like juniper berry, bay leaves and cloves, and in this recipe a considerable quantity of beer. The traditional recipe demands a cooking time of three to four hours in a large quantity of butter. We opt for only two hours and use a lot less butter. Our butcher in Amsterdam taught us to add the onions just for cooking and to take them out afterwards. This trick makes things a lot easier on your stomach.

Ingredients

1 kg lean stewing steak

flour, a handful

50 grams butter

750 grams shallots

4 tablespoons wine vinegar

750 ml beer

1 tablespoon sugar

2 bay leaves

3 cloves

6 juniper berries

2 small onions

2 slices wholemeal bread, crust removed

mustard

pepper

salt

Cut the meat into large pieces of about 3 cm. Put the meat in a plastic bag with a handful of flour and shake.

Take a heavy casserole and sear the pieces of meat in the butter over a high heat. Take out the meat and fry the peeled, whole shallots over a low heat. Next, add the meat to the shallots and then add the beer, sugar, some salt, bay leaves, cloves and juniper berries.

Smear the slices of bread with mustard, cut them in pieces and then add those to the stew as well. Let everything simmer for about two hours.

Cut the onions into pieces and only add those after an hour and a half. Take the whole shallots out when the dish is ready.

Serve the hash with potatoes or coarsely cut bread.

Wonderful chicken (with applesauce)
De allerlekkerste kip (met appelmoes)

A Dutch cookbook can't do without a recipe for chicken with applesauce. Only the very best chicken recipe, like the one our friend Lena tought us.

Ingredients

4 medium size chicken breasts
1 lemon
1 ½ onions
butter
125 ml whipping cream
1 tablespoon sour cream
2 cloves of garlic
a handful of fresh basil
1 dl white wine
1 tablespoon of ketchup
salt
pepper

Preheat the oven to 200 °C.

Cut the chicken breasts into four pieces. The pieces should not be too small or they will dry out in the oven. Put them in a dish. Squeeze out the juice of one lemon onto the chicken. Sprinkle with some salt and pepper and leave for 15 minutes.

Cut the onion into small pieces and brown it in a pan with a knob of butter on low flame.

Mix the whipping cream and the sour cream with the onions.

Press out 2 cloves of garlic. Finely chop the fresh basil. Add the garlic and half of the basil to the mixture in the pan. Add the white wine while stirring. Add the ketchup and keep stirring. Season with pepper and salt.

Pat the chicken breasts dry. Melt a knob of butter in a deep frying pan and fry the chicken breasts. Put them in the sauce as soon as they have browned on all sides. The chicken really has to be sealed or it will dry out. Put the chicken with sauce into an ovenproof dish and cover it with aluminium foil. Bake in the centre of the oven for half and hour. Mix in the remainder of the basil right before serving.

Serve with potatoes and applesauce.

Applesauce

Ingredients

1 kg cooking apples (Golden Reinettes)
125 grams sugar
1 bag of vanilla sugar (8 gr)
2 teaspoons cinnamon

The amount of sugar and cinnamon in this recipe can be adjusted to taste.
Peel apples, remove the cores, and cut them into small pieces.

Bring a little bit of water to the boil and put in the apples. Add sugar and vanilla sugar.

Bring everything to the boil again and leave the pan, covered, on a low heat, for half an hour. Mash the apples and season them with two teaspoons of cinnamon, or more.

Plaice with fennel
Schol met venkel

Plaice is one of the best-known types of fish in the Netherlands. The comparable flounder is actually better because it is somewhat firmer, but plaice is more readily available. Originally, baking fish in an oven ('stoven' in Dutch) was seen as a way to avoid the smell of fish frying in oil. It is however also a way to respect the subtle flavour of fish.

Ingredients

4 plaice (about 1 $\frac{1}{2}$ kg), cleaned
1 lemon
2 onions
olive oil
2 fennel tubers
2 tablespoons capers
500 grams tomatoes
slices of lemon
dill sprig
salt
pepper

Preheat the oven to 225 °C.

Rinse the plaice and pat them dry with a paper towel. Cut the lemon in half, sprinkle some juice onto the fish and leave it for 10 minutes.

Peel the onions and cut them into rings. Fry them in a little olive oil and put them aside.

Rinse the fennel, remove the bottom, and cut the rest in slices.

Grease an ovenproof dish with olive oil and put in the slices of fennel with a couple of tablespoons of water. Rub the plaice with salt and some olive oil, put them on top of the fennel and sprinkle with lemon juice. Put three quarters of the dill and the fried onion rings on top of the fish and add the capers.
Cut the tomatoes into slices, place them on top of the onion rings, dill and capers and sprinkle them with salt. Bake the dish in the oven for 25 minutes.

Serve with slices of lemon and the remainder of the dill.

Grilled herring
Gegrilde haring

May and June are the months for fresh 'maatjesharing',
young herring. This salted herring is sacred. Don't touch it.
Just eat it. The rest of the year this young herring is also
called white herring. Still delicious raw, but also suitable
for doing all kinds of things with. Grilled herring
resembles grilled sardines, but we find
they taste even better. Ideal for a large group!

Ingredients

(2 herrings per person is plenty)
8 fresh herrings
fresh dill
1 lemon
salt
freshly ground black pepper

Set the oven to grill and preheat it to 200 °C.

Make sure the herrings are not too wet. If necessary, pat them dry with a paper towel. Rub them with some salt and lavish with ground pepper.

Put the herrings on aluminium foil on a baking sheet and place them high up in the oven.

Turn the herrings over after about 5 minutes and grill the other side for 5 minutes.

Serve with dill and slices of lemon.

Vegetables

Nobody is surprised to see a box of strawberries at the greengrocer's in the middle of winter, while it is actually very strange indeed. We have grown so accustomed to greenhouse vegetables and products from countries far away that we hardly remember when which vegetables are harvested. Luckily, sometimes signs are put up in supermarkets that remind us that it's asparagus season, or that it's hotchpotch season. Most people are oblivious to the fact that there is also a courgette and a cauliflower season. Many people think that cauliflower is a typical winter vegetable, while it is actually at its best in the spring. Seasonal vegetables – grown outdoors or in unheated greenhouses – are tastier and often need fewer pesticides, and because they don't have to be flown in from far away they are also cheaper. Plenty of reason to check the vegetable calendar: harvest times for Dutch vegetables (see page 10).

Turnip tops and mustard cheese salad
Salade van raapstelen en mosterdkaas

The pale green turnip top leaves are the first leaves of the kohlrabi tuber or Chinese cabbage. An old-fashioned springtime vegetable packed with iron and vitamin C. They can be added to pasta or rice, stir-fried or used in soup and can even be used to make a delicious salad. In the Netherlands turnip tops are widely available from February to May.

Ingredients

200 grams turnip tops
200 grams mustard cheese
4 tablespoons olive oil
1 tablespoon sugar
1 clove of garlic
1 teaspoon tarragon
pepper
salt

Wash the turnip tops well with cold water. Remove the roots and hard ends and cut them into 5 cm pieces.

Dice the cheese and mix it through the turnip tops.

Prepare a vinaigrette with olive oil, lemon juice, 1 clove of pressed garlic, tarragon, pepper and salt. Whisk the vinaigrette with a fork for 1 minute; this makes it somewhat thicker. Pour it onto the salad right before serving.

Salsifies with sour cream
Schorseneren met crème fraîche

Salsifies are known as 'Poor man's asparagus' or 'Dutch winter asparagus'. Back in the days when salsifies were still common, they were also nicknamed 'kitchen maids' despair', because they were hell to clean. By scrubbing them first, then boiling and finally peeling them, you can save yourself lots of despair.

Ingredients

1 ½ kg salsifies
lemon juice
125 ml sour cream
a handful of fresh chives
pepper
salt

Bring a large pot of water to the boil.

Put the salsifies in water and scrub them clean with a brush.

Boil them for 5 minutes and then rinse in cold water. Peel the salsifies with a parer. Put them in a bowl of water and lemon juice to keep them white.

Bring a large pot with little water to the boil. As soon as the water is boiling place the salsifies in the pot and add some salt. Boil for 10 minutes.

Meanwhile, mix the sour cream with the chopped chives. Season with salt and freshly ground pepper.

Drain the salsifies and serve immediately with the sour cream.

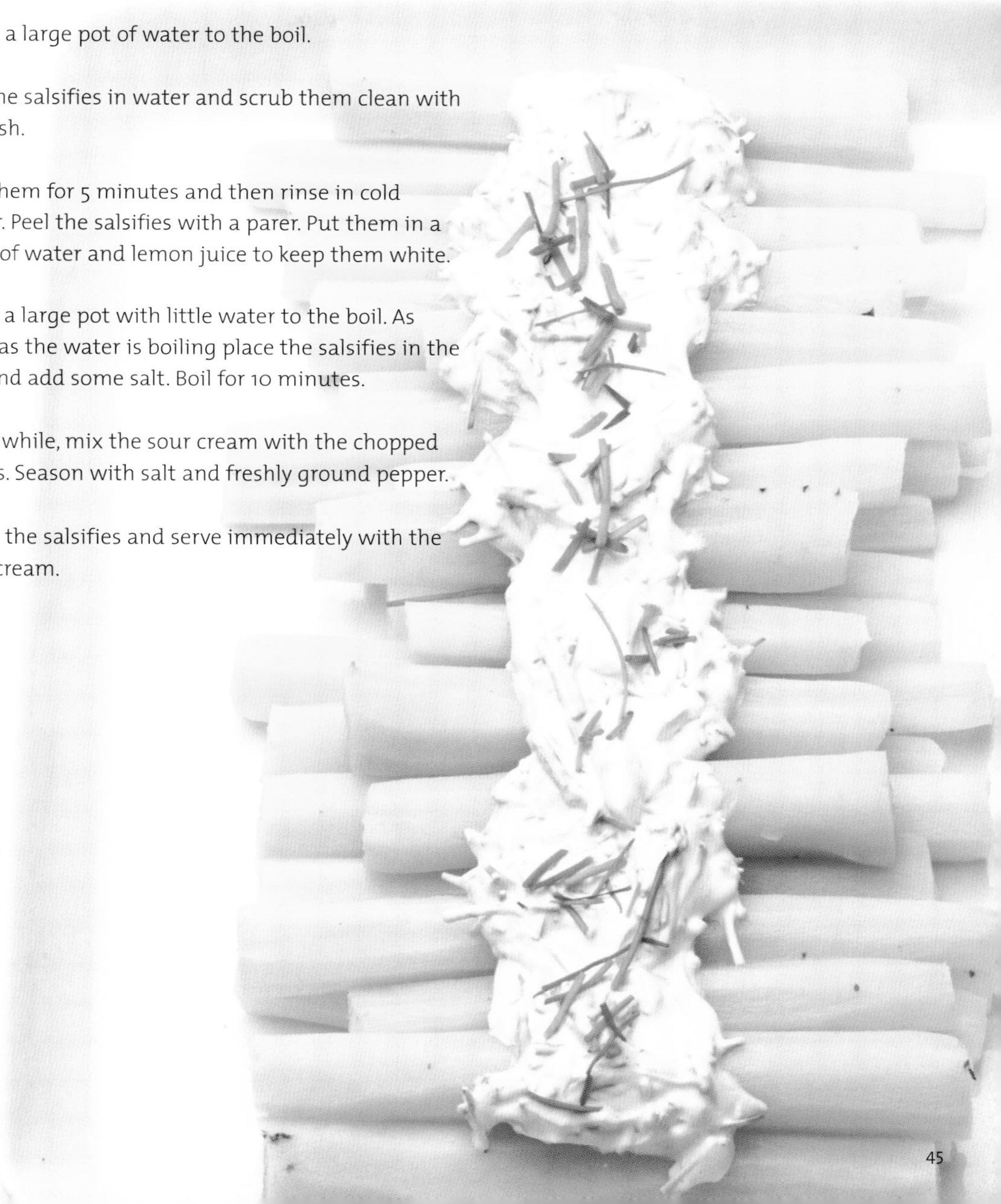

Steamed Brussels sprouts with garlic
Gestoomde spruitjes met knoflook

Choose small, young sprouts and buy them at a good greengrocer's or organic food shop.

Ingredients

750 grams Brussels sprouts	2 tablespoons balsamic vinegar
a handful of fresh parsley	salt
1 dl olive oil	pepper
3 cloves of garlic	

Bring a litre of water to the boil. Clean the Brussels sprouts. Remove the outer leaves and cut a slice off the bottom. Put the sprouts in a steamer and steam them for 10 minutes until they are al dente.

Prepare a vinaigrette with the olive oil, balsamic vinegar, pressed garlic, some pepper and salt and the finely chopped parsley.

Place the sprouts in a dish and pour the vinaigrette over them. Leave for about ten minutes and serve as a side dish.

Cauliflower with warm vinaigrette
Bloemkool met warme vinaigrette

This recipe is tastiest in spring when cauliflower is at its best.

Ingredients

1 cauliflower	100 ml white wine vinegar
1 knob of butter	a handful of fresh chives
3 cloves of garlic	freshly ground black pepper
1 dl olive oil	salt

Bring a large pot with a little water to the boil and add a little salt. Remove the stalk and the leaves. Wash the cauliflower and put it in the pot whole. Cover the pot and cook the cauliflower for about 10 minutes on a low heat until it is al dente.

Melt a knob of butter in the pan and add the pressed garlic. Add the olive oil and wine vinegar and add the chopped chives. Add some freshly ground black pepper and salt. Let it simmer on a low heat for a couple of minutes.
Place the cauliflower in a deep preheated dish and pour the warm vinaigrette over it. Serve as a side dish.

Beetroot with cream
Rode bieten met room

Young summer beetroots are the tastiest. They take an hour to cook. Older beetroots need to be cooked longer and are usually sold pre-cooked.

Ingredients

1 onion	vinegar
butter	2 tablespoons sour cream
4 cooked beetroots	salt
2 tablespoons sugar	pepper

Shred the onion, melt a knob of butter in the pan and brown the onions.

Cut the beetroots in small pieces. Heat them while stirring, with a knob of butter, sugar, vinegar and plenty of freshly ground pepper.

Add the onion to the beetroots and season with salt. Serve with sour cream

Sprout purée
Spruitjespuree

Sprout purée is eaten in small quantities as a side dish.

Ingredients

300 grams Brussels sprouts	nutmeg
200 grams floury potatoes	pepper
50 ml cream	salt

Clean the Brussels sprouts. Remove the outer leaves and cut a slice off the bottom. Bring to a boil in a litre of water. Pour off the water as soon as it is boiling – Pouring off the first batch of water keeps the sprouts from becoming bitter.

Bring a pot of water to the boil and add the potatoes. Add the sprouts after 5 minutes and let them cook for another 10 minutes until tender. Use a mixer to make an fluffy purée of the sprouts and potatoes and stir in the cream. Season with nutmeg, pepper and salt.

Parsnips
Pastinaken

Parsnips used to be a popular Dutch staple food before the potato appeared. This sweetish white tuber is still for sale at good Dutch greengrocers and in shops selling organic food.

Ingredients

800 grams parsnips
2 tablespoons lemon juice
2 tablespoons flour
50 grams butter
1 dl chicken stock
1 teaspoon ground nutmeg
100 grams grated Old Amsterdam
    cheese
pepper
salt

Preheat the oven to 250 ºC.

Peel the parsnips, cut them lengthwise and then in 1 to 2 cm slices.

Bring a pot with ample water to the boil and add some salt, lemon juice and two tablespoons of flour. Whisk the flour in a little cold water before adding it; this avoids lumps. Add the parsnips and boil them over a high heat for 5 minutes.

Melt the butter in a casserole and add the stock, nutmeg and some salt and pepper. Drain the parsnips in a colander and add them to the casserole. Braise for 5 minutes.

Alternate layers of parsnips and sauce in a greased ovenproof dish. Sprinkle some grated Old Amsterdam cheese on top of every layer.
Bake in the middle of the oven for 15 minutes.

Serve with meat or fish.

Stewed pears
Stoofpeer

Stewing pears are served as a hot desert or as a main course or side dish. There are no longer many varieties of stewing pears available in the Netherlands and you will mainly find the Gieser Wildeman variety. Ask your greengrocer for suggestions. In any case, it is useless to use dessert pears, as they are far too soft. Pears are not naturally as pink as shown here. Heating the pears slowly makes them go pinkish, but we used a few drops of red food colouring. This does no harm, unlike the food colourings that were available in the past, but is not mandatory for the taste of this side dish. This recipe uses red currant juice.

Ingredients

5 stewing pears (Gieser Wildeman variety)
4 cloves
wine vinegar
lemon peel
100 ml red currant juice
150 grams sugar
juice of $\frac{1}{2}$ a lemon
salt

Put the pears in a pot of water on the stove. The pears must be completely covered or they will not turn pink evenly. Add the cloves, salt, vinegar and a strip of lemon peel to the pears. Stew the pears for one hour over a very low heat. Now add the red currant juice and the sugar and continue to stew for half an hour.

Carefully lift the pears out of the pot (don't pick them up by their stalks!) and sprinkle them with the lemon juice. Serve hot.

Stewed apples with lemon
Gestoofde appeltjes met citroen

We used to have an apple tree in our garden. If you have your own apple tree, you'll know that you have to be very creative to find ways of processing all those boxes of apples. After stuffing ourselves with applesauce, baked apples and apple pies we moved to stewed apples. This recipe is the one we liked best, not too sweet and with plenty of lemon.

Ingredients

1 kg cooking apples (Golden Reinettes)
juice of 1/2 lemon
6 cloves
ground cinnamon
3 tablespoons sugar
1 tablespoon vanilla sugar
juice of 1/2 a lemon
strips of lemon peel

Peel the apples, remove the cores, and cut them in eighths. Sprinkle them with a little lemon juice.

Bring a large pot with 3 dl water to the boil. Add the cloves, 3 teaspoons of ground cinnamon, sugar, the juice of half a lemon, and six strips of lemon peel.

Put the apple segments in the pot and cover for 10 minutes on a low heat. Uncover every now and then to check that they aren't getting too mushy.

Garnish with some strips of lemon peel and extra cinnamon. Serve as a side dish with meat or hotchpotch.

Bare buttocks in the field
Blote billetjes in 't veld

This dish – a combination of French beans and haricot beans – is traditionally eaten on New Year's Day. After all the 'oliebollen' (a kind of doughnuts) and drink this is a pleasantly sober dish which combines well with smoked sausage. Apart from the name 'Bare buttocks in the field' you may also come across the names 'Bare buttocks in the green', 'Naked children on the grass' or 'Bare little men in the field'. Dried haricot beans are best, but a jar/tin of baked beans will do as well.

Ingredients

200 grams dried haricot beans
2 bay leaves
2 cloves
1 onion
400 grams French beans
1 clove of garlic
pepper
salt

Soak the haricot beans for 8 to 24 hours in water with the bay leaves, the cloves, the onion and some salt. Then boil them in the same water for 45 minutes until cooked.

String the French beans. They only need 15 to 20 minutes to cook so wait for a while until you put them on so that everything will be ready at the same time. Add some salt while boiling.

After the French beans have boiled, cut them into 2 cm diamonds and mix them with the haricot beans.

Brown the finely chopped garlic and add it to the dish. Season the vegetables with pepper and salt.

'Bare buttocks in the field' is also often prepared as a hotchpotch. To do so, use 2 kilos of floury potatoes and mix with the above ingredients.

Warm kohlrabi, caper and coriander salad
Warme salade van koolrabi, kappertjes en koriander

Kohlrabi is a delicacy that is hardly eaten anymore in the Netherlands. It is the tuber of the cabbage plant and grows above ground. Kohlrabi is available almost all year round, from early spring to late autumn. Kohlrabi is not the same as a swede, which grows underground. There are two kinds of kohlrabi: big and small. Choose the small one for this salad.

Ingredients

750 grams kohlrabi
3 spring onions
fresh coriander, a handful
lemon juice
$\frac{1}{2}$ dl olive oil
1 tablespoon mustard
2 tablespoons capers
salt
pepper

In a pot, bring a little water to the boil with some salt.

Remove the leaves from the kohlrabi and put them aside. Peel the kohlrabi with a peeler and cut it into pieces. Boil the pieces with the leaves for 10 minutes until they are al dente.

Cut the spring onions into rings and finely chop the coriander.

Put the juice of half a lemon in a cup. Add some salt and pepper. Whisk the lemon juice with a fork and slowly pour in the olive oil. Keep whisking as this makes the vinaigrette somewhat thicker. Add half a tablespoon of mustard and whisk.

Put the kohlrabi and the leaves together with the spring onions and coriander in a dish. Carefully stir in the vinaigrette and sprinkle with capers. Serve while the salad is still warm.

Sweet

Dutch people love sweet things.
We actually eat more sweets than any
other European European country.
On weekdays the Dutch usually enjoy
a simple desert like yoghurt or 'vla',
a creamy, flavored custard sold in
cartons. But there is also a strong
tradition of home-made desserts.

'Haagse bluf' (strawberry fool)

The name 'Haagse bluf' (Hague bluff) originates from a prejudice that citizens of The Hague tended to put on airs. Sometimes people referred to the city's coat of arms, which depicted a stork as: 'High on its legs, thinly feathered and with a big mouth'. The desert is traditionally made with red currant juice but we prefer it mixed with strawberry sauce and served with fresh strawberries. The strawberry sauce can be bought or homemade from blended fresh strawberries.

Ingredients
lemon juice
2 egg whites
100 grams granulated sugar
150 ml strawberry sauce
box of fresh strawberries

Rub a large bowl with lemon juice to remove any traces of grease. Whisk the egg whites in the bowl with an electric mixer until they peak. You should be able to turn the bowl upside-down without spilling.
Then whisk in the sugar and slowly pour in the strawberry sauce. Keep whisking. Serve this desert in small servings with fresh strawberries.
Strawberry fool is made with raw eggs.
Make sure that the eggs are very fresh and serve the strawberry fool immediately. It is not recommended for pregnant women, children and the elderly.

Tip
Don't buy your strawberries too early in the season. in the Netherlands strawberries only really start tasting like strawberries in May.

'Poffertjes' (mini-pancakes) with forest fruits

'Poffertjes' are especially a children's and tourists' favourite, though they can certainly be eaten as a desert, with ice cream or fresh fruits. To make poffertjes you really need a poffertjespan.

Ingredients
5 grams dried yeast
100 grams flour
100 grams buckwheat flour
2 eggs
$^1/_2$ teaspoon salt
3 dl lukewarm milk
butter
300 grams fresh forest fruits
    (blackberries, raspberries,
    blueberries)
icing sugar to taste

Let the yeast dissolve in a bowl with 1 tablespoon of milk.

Put the buckwheat flour in a bowl and stir in the eggs, the yeast, the salt and half the milk. Whisk it with a whisk or fork until there are no lumps left. Add the rest of the milk and stir until the batter is nice and smooth.

Cover the bowl of batter with a damp cloth and leave in a warm spot for an hour.

Heat up the 'poffertjes' griddle and grease it using a brush with butter (a paper towel will do as well).

Pour the batter in the hollows of the griddle. Fry the 'poffertjes' over a medium-high heat and carefully turn them with a fork or pricker.

Serve the 'poffertjes' on a preheated plate and put the rinsed forest fruit on top of them. Sprinkle with icing sugar to taste.

Even more delicious than icing sugar is a few scoops of whipped cream on top of the forest fruits.

Rice pudding
Rijstebrij

The rice used for rice pudding in the past was a round-grained white rice. Nowadays, pudding and desert rice are available. As children, we ate rice pudding made with left-over rice. A good choice is (unseasoned) risotto rice, which is in-between very mushy dessert rice and the long grain of ordinary rice. Influenced by the Italian kitchen we would like to depart from traditional recipes, where sugar is only added after serving. Cooking the sugar with the rice and adding a lot of lemon peel imbues the rice pudding with an extra dimension.

Boil the milk in a pot with as thick a bottom as possible. Add the rice and some salt, bring to the boil, turn down the heat and keep a close eye on it. Nothing is more annoying than burnt rice pudding. Add the sugar, the cinnamon stick and the grated lemon and allow the mixture to simmer in a covered pot for 45 minutes.

Meanwhile, using a *zester* or thin knife, cut very thin strips of lemon peel and let them dry for a moment – this makes them go curly.

Serve the hot rice pudding with cinnamon, a knob of butter and some lemon peel curls.

Ingredients

1 litre full cream milk
125 grams risotto rice
a pinch of salt
50 grams sugar
1 cinnamon stick
2 teaspoons grated lemon peel
lemon peel
ground cinnamon
a knob of butter

'Hang up' with prunes
Hangop met pruimen

'Hang up' is a curd made by hanging yoghurt or buttermilk in a tea towel or a piece of cheesecloth and letting it drain. Hence the Dutch name 'Hangop'. You can also put a tea towel on top of a colander and pour the buttermilk or yoghurt on to it. Yoghurt hang up tends to become very thick whereas buttermilk hang up is somewhat lighter. Due to Dutch buttermilk not being as thick as it used to be you will need quite a lot of it.

Put a colander in a deep dish, place a clean tea towel on top of it it and pour in yoghurt or buttermilk until it is filled to the rim. Let it drip for at least three hours while re-filling it. Stir every now and then if it does not drip through properly.

Half an hour before serving heat the wine, the juice of an orange and some orange peel shavings in a frying pan. Add the prunes, the sugar, the vanilla pod and the spices. Heat thoroughly until most of the liquid has evaporated. Make sure to leave some of the syrupy liquid to serve with the hang up and the fragrant prunes.

Ingredients

2 litres yoghurt or 4 litres
    buttermilk
200 ml red wine
juice of 1 orange
250 grams pitted prunes
50 grams sugar
1 vanilla pod
ginger powder
nutmeg

Spiced gingerbread
Kruidkoek

Every remote corner of the Netherlands has its own spiced gingerbread. Diest, Deventer, Drachten and Dokkum all have their own recipes. The secret lies in the specific amounts of spices that are used. The best fun of all is experimenting with pepper, ginger, nutmeg and cloves.

Ingredients

200 grams butter
1 pinch of salt
4 teaspoons ginger powder
4 teaspoons cinnamon
1 teaspoon ground cloves
$\frac{1}{2}$ teaspoon black pepper
$\frac{1}{2}$ teaspoon ground nutmeg
150 grams soft (dark) brown sugar
3 eggs
200 grams flour
butter to grease the pan

Preheat the oven to 160 °C.

Heat the butter in a pan. Mix salt, ginger, cinnamon, cloves, pepper and nutmeg with the soft brown sugar and the melted butter.

Beat the eggs and add them.

Slowly add the flour to the mixture and whisk it to a smooth batter.

Grease a cake tin and fill it with the batter. Place it just a little under the centre of the oven and bake the cake for about 1 hour 15 minutes, until done. Leave it to cool in the tin.

Apple pie
Appeltaart

Apple pie is a national pride in the Netherlands. Recipes are often passed on from generation to generation. The oldest recipe for apple pie that we came across was in a book called *Een notabel boecxken van cokeryen* (A notable little cookery book, approx. 1514) and it was hardly different from the recipes known to us today. Our apple pie is a generous one, with two kilos of apples and a whole lot of raisins. It takes quite a birthday party to finish it off. The Netherlands' best apple pie is sold at lunch café 'Winkel' which can be found on the corner of the Noordermarkt and the Westerstraat in Amsterdam. After a lengthy period of spying in and around their shop, we discovered that they make their pies with Red Boskoop apples. Remember that name.

Ingredients

300 grams large yellow sultanas
500 grams self-rising flour
2 eggs
300 grams cold butter
175 grams soft brown sugar
pinch of salt
peel of $\frac{1}{2}$ a lemon
2 kilos Red Boskoop apples
juice of $\frac{1}{2}$ a lemon
75 grams soft brown sugar
6 teaspoons cinnamon

Steep the raisins in lukewarm water for 10 minutes. Preheat the oven to 175 °C.

Put the flour in a mixing bowl. Beat the eggs. Save a little of the beaten egg to brush over the dough at a later stage. Mix the rest through the flour.

Cube the cold butter and add to the flour mixture, with the sugar, some salt and the grated lemon peel. Knead the dough until smooth and leave for 15 minutes in a cool place.

Peel the apples, dice them and mix with the raisins, lemon juice sugar and cinnamon.

Grease a springform pan and use three quarters of the dough to cover the bottom and the sides. Let the dough hang over the rim a little. Put in the apple mixture and press with both hands.

Use the rest of the dough to make thick cables and lay them crosswise over the filling. With wet hands the strings can be kneaded like clay. Fold in the protruding edges of the pie and brush the dough with egg.
Place the apple pie low down in the oven and bake for about 1 hour until done. Let the pie cool in the springform pan until the crust is firm.

Index

With thanks to...

We would like to thank our test panel for all the hours they spent cooking hotchpotch and sprouts in order to try out all the recipes time and again, and also for the recipes they gave us.

Anna Luten and Michael Krass
Hanneke van der Horst
Elizabeth Klønhammer
Anne Leiss
Liesbeth van der Maat
Chris Mitchell
Gonnie Mulder
Irene Muller
Guus van Nifterik
Marijke van Oordt
Marjolijn van Oordt
Josien Piek
Amber van Rijn
Paulien Schoof
Marijke Sikkel
Dirk, Ariadne and Felix Snoodijk
Lena Träff
Charlotte Venema
Marion Witter
The test panel at Uitgeverij Gottmer
Photo studio Gerhard Witteveen: Gerhard, Moniek, Piroschka and Marloes
ICATT interactive media

We would also like to thank the many shopkeepers who helped us in our quest for good quality Dutch products. The quality and attention from greengrocers, butchers and other shopkeepers proved how indispensible they are time and again.

We thank & Klevering Zuid (Jacob Obrechtstraat 19a, Amsterdam) for lending us their plates and dishes.